Electricity "Transport Trains"— slipping information under our noses into our lives

Some secrets of how we get roped into the universe's scenes and stories

Margaret A. Harrell

Paperback ISBN: 979-8-9860526-9-4
Hardcover ISBN: 979-8-9860526-8-7

A Published in Heaven Series Book

Published in Heaven Books include titles by His Holiness The Dalai Lama,
President Jimmy Carter, Thomas Merton, Seamus Heaney, Hunter S.
Thompson, Jack Kerouac, Andy Warhol, Allen Ginsberg, Yoko Ono, William S.
Burroughs, Edvard Munch, Diane di Prima, Jim Carroll, Amiri Baraka, Gregory
Corso, John Updike, Rita Dove, Wendell Berry, David Amram, Douglas Brinkley,
BONO, Ron Whitehead, Lawrence Ferlinghetti, and many more.

Published in conjunction with Saeculum University Press of Sibiu, Romania,
and Raleigh, North Carolina

For inquiries, signed copies, and speaking requests,
contact marharrell@hotmail.com
https://margaretharrell.com

Front cover image and design: Grant Goodwine, https://grantgoodwine.bigcartel.com/
Interior and back cover design: Deborah Perdue, https://illuminationgraphics.com/

CONTENTS

Author's Note

It was soon after I moved into my new house, the first one I'd owned. My sister and her husband were helping me hang a picture. I held the little machine that detected electricity. Oops. There it was in the wall. Oops. There too. My sister took over. The same thing. My brother-in-law thought it was impossible. So he took the little gadget. Guess what. No electricity! So my sister and I had enough electricity in our hands that the machine detected it in the walls when we held it.

Everybody has electricity. It just depends on how much. But we all have it, like we have arms and legs. Yet I know of not many people who have has asked this question, *Well, does our electricity communicate with the electricity in the universe?*

Duh. Wouldn't we expect it? How would it not occur? Wouldn't two like things exchange information!!!!???? Oh no. That would mean . . .!!!!!!!!!! The electricity in the universe, in our TV sets, in our computer programs that fueled everything we did—that very same element surrounded our brains and sometimes chattered away with those brains.

Oh no!!!!!!! How is it possible we never thought of it, just as we for centuries never had the thought that little creatures carried germs that made us sick. We thought it "just happened." Or it happened in some superstitious fashion.

So let's dive down into our relationship to the universe's creative impulse, creative energy—the energy that can move mountains, can explode cities—through our common affinity for and content of . . . ELECTRICITY. Our electrical nature, which Goethe hinted at in his phrase "elective affinity," that featured in a classic he wrote where a couple, Edouard and Charlotte, meet Ottilie, and Charlotte and Ottilie unexpectedly fall in love. They refrain from any physical steps to consummate the attraction. Even so, the plot acts out the theory that certain chemicals attract each other. Consequently, which man did her child's eyes, the window of the soul, look like? The one she had an affinity with so strong that in Goethe's plot the infant created in her marriage yet carried the eyes of the spiritual lover. Oh no!!!! That would be the end of us if we couldn't even tell where physical items, events, people came from. But that's not the topic of this book. Let's start with what we can assure the reader is true and accurate.

INTRODUCTION

There was a time . . . when I woke every morning to a room filled with guides . . . there was a time when all I had to do was stumble or walk over to the computer and sit. Then stay there for hours: writing, striking out, adding, . . . ah, printing . . . for hours the computer printouts awed me with their impossible changes from what was on the screen—picking out an isolated set of words to print, ignoring the rest. But when I printed the same page again, what zoomed out of the printer? A different set of words. Lifting the words it chose to highlight, ignoring the rest, it set up a new focus— in each instance, the text chosen was different. Nothing survived one round. No page, once printed, looked like it did the time before. It was omitting content. *There was no such thing as a duplicate.* There was only Focus. And Refocus. A small set of words on the page had center stage—For Now. Only Now.

Taking a bow, occupying my awareness, that focus was then gone, pouf, as the next words stepped forth, onto the page, or the next graphic arrangement that squeezed text into a design. Ah, those days my unconscious had nothing else to be busied with. It was a serious job. And yet . . . very few people have seen these productions, this ten years of work. In fact, supervised work if I do say so, because the room was abuzz with spirit energy. I offer some of the productions and insights now, leaving behind piles of pages, printouts of versions of published books with the computer PK participation, for this effort. Here is a picture of ten years of my life.

If you are floating in the middle of a lake you could create vibrations in the water and if there were an astute person on the shore they can read these vibrations and (provided he can decode their meaning) you can send information to him. When we speak to others the same thing happens—our voice box creates a certain pattern in air (a sound wave) and the listener's ears receives these patterns and interprets the information.

With light or electricity you can create a wave / modulation. These can be done at a very high frequency so they carry a lot of data. The receiver at the other end can read these modulations and interpret the message.[1]

PART ONE

Electrical Imagination— plots we walk into propagated in the universe

So, through a long-ago recurring initiation I had, that science has not even now caught up with, I am dealing with how electricity that we harness into TV story dynamics actually is "contagious"—it "hops" off the set into real-life settings. **That is, it is not after a certain point programmed by us. It doesn't stop at the end of where we are using it. It keeps "moving." We should have guessed. Since it never stops, how could we think harnessing it into TV sets "stopped it"? Oh, mistaken notion of the wise.**

✳

The electromagnetic radiation of light energy, a wavelength, is "a type of kinetic energy."[2] That is, it travels.

OK, so now we have that out of the way. To produce photons, atoms "heat up."

And Light energy is "kinetic—in motion. AND visible. To us.

But it has some invisible actions up its sleeve. That's what I stumbled onto.

Some ideas in this book, I got introduced to in a spiritual initiation in 1985. Now, decades and many, many experiences later, it all makes sense. But most people didn't have this initiation, so as I share it, it may illuminate a few light bulbs for a few (or many?) people.

Finding information slipped to us in unexpected places, some of it carried on electric wires into TV sets—continuing its activity when we turn our thoughts elsewhere—is a principle I witnessed and am depicting here.

Our Cells are specialized to conduct electrical currents. Electricity is required for the nervous system to send signals throughout the body and to the brain, making it possible for us to move, think and feel.

—Amber Plante,
"How the Human Body Uses Electricity"

A responsibility of light: information transport

Electrical Information

Trains of thought in the literal sense;
only, they are image trains, kinetic energy
trains intersecting with thought and
transforming it into action.
Oh no. Oh yes.

I am listening to the TV, and—! My hand begins vibrating. (Good, it's the right.) This lets me know electricity has "found" me. The scene on TV has now "connected" with me. The science that established the technology is silent here. It has not posited a theory that even looks at this next development.

A pattern is at work. A kinetic pattern we see on the TV scene. Is there such a thing as kinetic patterns? Of course. From long ago I began using the phrase "symbolic actions," meaning that an action can have a symbolic dimension that is imbued with energetic power. By affinity, by similarity, this pattern has "hopped" through the wires and glass over to me. Invisibly, mind you. No one has a clue about and glass over to me. Invisibly, mind you. No one has a clue about these things. At least, no one in this 3-D dimension is speaking up about it, that I know of.

Here's how it works, in case you are hanging on your seat. The pattern finds a similarity, perhaps a weakness, in me, or it could be a potential strength it will reinforce. It is looping out, latching on to resonances. Ah. There's one. In me. I'm fine with that if it's positive. But connecting me invisibly to a scene in the TV that connects to my imminent future—by sharing a pattern pictorially—the energy of the pattern or just the configuration (the dynamics of character and plot) will find a new location. The kinetic quality of the light looking to reproduce the scene. Why not there, in my life in a day or a few days? As if it can read into the future, this kinetic factor in this "future" scene *is seen, by consciousness*, in the light of the prior TV one NOW and intensifies through it. That can be helpful. Or terribly distorted. Augmentation is at work. Augmentation is a factor in our world we take little account of. Dreams use it, though, a step ahead or in a sidestep.

Suppose it's a negative scene and connects to another human.

Suppose, in fact, it's what I call "negative electricity," in, while intensifying, misreading me. *A gigantic oops.* If that happens, a huge power is operating in a negative, misinterpretation field.

It can, though, be a positive field.

So, there are *subtle* electrical grids that most of us—practically all—are unaware of. The sort that kinetically combines with us, as visible light enters into its invisible replication system, joining with and hijacking those of our creations that operate through electrical transmission—applying, amplifying the TV scene one might be looking at innocently—identifying with emotionally perhaps, not having the experience, as I do, of noticing the exact moment the connection takes hold, latches on. Locks on. The "warhead" now aiming at its target. I feel it in the electrical shaking of my hand or my leg. Thus, at least having advance notice.

Woefully unconscious, most of us never suspect that this grid is part of our Cause.

To Be Clear, as this is all so new

A TV scene "look-alike" that might otherwise have played out in my life in low key is now set to "barnstorm in." Connections are at work across a plastic timeline or non-time line

These *subtle* electrical grids, most of us—practically all—are unaware of.

Who notices, if anyone, the *exact* moment the intensity particle "connects"—now locked onto its target? The target being a scene in my very own life. Or yours. All in the unconscious. Why didn't we realize that the universe was visual? Artistic? That it put together this scene and its likeness, in a vulnerable individual? That it too has a process for reproducing itself.

Or sometimes there is no TV, just a distant scene (in configuration) my own energy is locking into. By getting this signal, I at least have advance notice.

For the TV set is not the end of it. It can also happen through books and other modes of conveying "live" patterns to us. Perhaps less often? I'm not sure. Rather like germs before their discovery, in our physical energy.

STUART: . . . If you go down in scale, much much smaller than atoms, below the level of matter, as things get smaller and smaller, everything would be sort of smooth and featureless, until twenty-five orders of magnitude smaller than atoms you get to the very bottom level called the Planck scale, where there's some kind of patterns, coarseness, geometry, information. [Fascinating] . . .

STUART: *We don't really know what to call it, at this most basic level of quantum gravity. But somehow, Planck scale geometry gives rise to irreducible features in physics, like mass, spin and charge. And also qualia, we think. The precursors of consciousness, or consciousness itself, may be actually embedded in Planck scale geometry, just like spin, mass, and charge that give rise to the material world. In other words, the essential features of consciousness are built into the universe at its most basic level, and repeat in scale holographically, so qualia become accessible to quantum biology in the brain.* [emphasis added][3]

Introducing the Narrator

Sometimes one's whole life is an exercise in memory. And one can only get to where one can start, by reaching the memory point one starts from. Detouring all the while, until—

Such a detour, *in the context of the total self*, I have lived—you might say we all have.

I didn't start from where she (my formerly most evolved self) stopped. And she didn't need me to remember unless I insisted. Insisting, I reached some of the memory. A memory that was an energy. Or vice versa. An energy that was a container.

Such is the end of a detour. It had seemed to be going into another direction. A brand-new detour. But something felt wrong. But seeing this hodgepodge, this misstep from the past, I wanted to go back to it, see how it would look, undetoured from, but stepped straight out of. Not that it would necessarily mean anything to anyone else; they would have their own degrees, longitudes and latitudes of detour, carved out, from within their own consciousness. I had to get through this; to go on, from the point and moment of **the Initiation in Zurich.** Square One.

I and "the Initiator," a cosmic spirit guide (though I had a more personal name for him), were writing literature together—pure art, from my point of view—but, he insisted, I had to remove all negative energy from the text. The guide used a technique that did this. The consciousness came in, eliminating the negative energy in the writing. Taking it *from each page.* But as it (the removed energy) went out, it could strike someone like lightning, who was vulnerable to the DISCARD; i.e., like "nuclear waste," these discards of removed, rejected negative energy in the words (or was it patterns? Intentions?) could, with unfortunate consequences, resonate with someone down on himself (or herself), someone in a negative frame of mind. There was no way around it.

However, here is where I learned that if, by chance, someone did resonate with and embrace the departing pattern of negative energy—that was invisible in the air—there was no way to AVOID letting this become an encounter with "their own karma"; that is, if someone walked into the discard, which was not completely de-energized, as it was removed in striking out words.

This meant an unwitting person—vulnerable to THE MISTAKE IT REPRESENTED—could encounter that mistake, lifted out of the pages of the book being revised, IN PURE ENERGY. I WAS TAUGHT THAT. I did not have—nor did the earth have, at that time—either the position, the authority, the credibility, or the opportunity to MAKE IT OTHERWISE. Besides, I was seeing it myself, as a new instruction in energy laws. A principle, not known. Not before, so far as I then remembered. Oh, how the veils hang heavy and hard before we learn what we know, who we are. Energy worked like that. This level of it did. The level where I fit, I guess. We will see. I *began* that day, that day in Zurich. I was born then, the first step.

IN TIENEN, BELGIUM: Fast forward ten years . . .

Let's keep these fast forwards up. First, going back, then quickly reaching today . . .

in this Book on Computer PK.

How much information is out there that we don't sense?

How can information be squeezed into transport—on telephone wires, cables—but not go hither and yon or through human minds? How can it be herded like sheep and, in no instance, stampede over a cliff? How can it be whipped like slaves or jailed prisoners to stay "in line"—and not escape at "random"? Or can it? Can the human mind stand up and say: *Wait a moment—count me in?* Does the human mind decide to be "part of the action"? Why not? And if so, how?

There are rumors and anecdotes about people getting their awareness intertwined with machines. Take a famous example in science. Physicist Wolfgang Pauli had the reputation of causing such chaos electronically that even being in proximity to a high-powered lab, he shut the machines down without conscious intent. Be it in a train station in town or in the building, he caused machine breakdown, resulting in nonfunctioning oscilloscopes, machines on fire, etc. No explanation ever found, except "the Pauli effect." But what "effect"? Presumably the oddity obeyed that rule we lived by: cause/effect. However mysterious the cause was, if it was a "cause," then it obeyed the universal law: "cause/effect."

Staying with this presumption, how did the information—the "order," the "intent," no matter if it was mechanical—travel? And what does Light have to do with it? Does information travel through light? Of course, it does. It travels through electricity. Ah ha. Energy is interchangeable with mass. Is energy interchangeable somehow with information? Is information interchangeable with mass? That is, suppose all mass has information—that makes sense—then what is information hiding when we exert energy?

Not that I got the idea here, but "In 2019, physicist Melvin Vopson of the University of Portsmouth proposed that information is equivalent to mass and energy, existing as a separate state of matter, a conjecture known as the mass-energy-information equivalence principle. This would mean that every bit of information has a finite and quantifiable mass."[4]

How does information give us and take from us energy? Can it—information that we have no knowledge of—heal us? Make us sick? Help us get out of bed in glee? Well, obviously yes. We can, in my case—or could—like a rainmaker calling the rain, tell the computer, "Print me a surprise!"

I'm sitting at the computer. Or was. All through the 1990s in my apartment in Belgium. I know it will happen because it's predictable. Science likes that—it must be following some system. Some "cause." Of course, science doesn't theoretically believe in my "effect." (Well, some quantum-mind or consciousness proponents would if they knew.) But no matter. Let's go on. I write a paragraph for my book, whatever one I'm in at that moment. Wham. I punch print. Using my technique of inertia—

> Mass is that quantity that is solely dependent upon the inertia of an object. The more inertia that an object has, the more mass that it has. A more massive object has a greater tendency to resist changes in its state of motion. . . .

Suppose that there are two seemingly identical bricks at rest on the physics lecture table. Yet one brick consists of mortar and the other brick consists of Styrofoam. Without lifting the bricks, how could you tell which brick was the Styrofoam brick? You could give the bricks an identical push in an effort to change their state of motion. The brick that offers the least resistance is the brick with the least inertia—and therefore the brick with the least mass (i.e., the Styrofoam brick).[5]

Using the split-second shift from idle (in inertia) to active printer (receiving sudden energy), I click the printer on/off/on. It starts. It "gulps." It sputters. Starts up again. Whamo. A strange page comes out—reconfigured. Nothing like what's on the screen. A surprise.

And I *feel* the energy. My own mind delights, adding a new energy—of amazement, delight, invigoration. We are one, me and the computer. And then I look to see what came out.

I suppose—since no one else is supposing—that that moment when the printer went from still to motion, when it revved up, gave the computer PK its chance. It leapt into the instant of shift, the high energy of on/off, and *directed it*. Hijacked it. And whamo. The computer created. It suddenly became "a creator." Or someone did. Spirits, you say? OK. If the reader believes in the afterlife or beforelife, the spirit world, then the answer is easy.

It knew these principles. Easy principles, once explained. And coopted the energy of the "in between" that came in from a timeless "location." It intercepted the latent, potential energy, unused by us Earthlings, who did not know it was there to call on. So once I saw the PK action begin, I joined in. Full force. Full blazing intention ahead.

Initially, this process started out small. But over ten years, 1991–2001, it grew more and more elaborate—like a skilled graphic designer, inserting illustrations made from text variations in my books but occasionally reconfiguring personal letters. Not shy, either, if an observer was in the room. So I had my occasional observers sign a witness note. (Two had PhDs.)

Pioneer of non-equilibrium thermodynamics Viscount Ilya Prigogine showed that what we take to be purely determinate (i.e., linear) systems can periodically enter into brief periods of *radical instability* ("the instability phase"), at which point they become essentially unpredictable.

> What happens *after* the system emerges out of the instability phase cannot be guessed at—many possible pathways exist . . . The instability phase is the fulcrum about which the universe turns . . .[6]

This was alternately called, by Prigogine, "bundles of converging trajectories." [7] Imagine the freedom that opens up. My computer did. And it and I saw eye to eye. Explore. See what's "out there." They had, moreover, he underlined, undiscernibility.

"**Without** the instability phase (during which no deterministic pathways are ordained)," explains "The Information Universe," "the only type of information in the universe would be information of the 'confirmation' variety." But this is no information at all (as it has no frame of reference to confirm!), "so what we'd end up with in this (purely hypothetical) case would be **an utterly sterile universe . . .** a closed universe, a universe which is made up entirely of redundancy, a recycled universe, a universe which repeats itself *ad nauseam* . . ."[8]

Now, given this vociferous defense by so worthy a pioneer physicist, I was being of service to the universe, helping it move ahead—not be static, redundant, repetitive, recycling itself, which it wasn't. No, I was helping it reinvent itself. Helping it show us some of its tricks. Our minds could "get it," understand. Mine did. We only had to show them. That is, the open ones.

PART TWO

Examples Galore
Handbook of Computer PK

1991 to 2001—Belgium, USA

The proof. The proof. Where is it?

Considering how difficult it is—and perhaps uninteresting—to just pick pages out of context, out of a book (or even a letter), to give examples of the computer creations during printing, I decided to use this space to introduce the last books that contained such illustrations. And they contained a lot. That's *Space Encounters: Chunking Down the Twenty-first Century* I and II and *Space Encounters* III: *Inserting Consciousness into Collisions*—which is *this* book's theme. Everything collides. Usually it slips by. We pay no notice. All the time, things touch. It's a major sense of ours: to touch. But meetings are actually exchange points. Change points.

What does "particles collide" mean?

The Large Hadron Collider has a seventeen-mile circumference. It has the title of largest on the planet.

But the latter fraction of its name is a little misleading. That's because what collides in the LHC are the tiny pieces inside the hadrons, not the hadrons themselves . . .

In particle physics [high energy physics], the term "collide" can mean that two protons *glide through* each other, and their fundamental components pass so close together that they can talk to each other . . . [my emphasis]

In *Symmetry Magazine*, Sarah Charley explains that "this subatomic symbiosis . . . [is] not restricted to the laboratory environment; particles are also accelerated by cosmic sources such as supernova remnants. 'This happens everywhere in the universe,' [Richard] Ruiz [Durham University theorist] says. 'The LHC and its experiments are not special in that sense. They're more like a big concert hall that provides the energy to pop open and record the symphony inside each proton.' " [9]

So it's the 1990s. Let me set the stage. I'm sitting at the computer, punch print, and—this comes out.

CONTENTS

83V　　≡♥£

Consternation?

No. I'm elated. Flying out afterwards as I wait with baited breath is this "other half." Now the whole image on the computer screen is complete. Only, it's adjusted, split, rearranged, no longer a mere Contents page but something highly visually creative:

Gener

Introd

Prolo

That's easy to put together.

CONTENTS

Gener

Introd

Prolog

Thanks,

83V   ≡♥£

A perfect fit, as if someone ripped the on-screen image in two and put one half on one sheet, the other half on the other. Don't ask me how.

Now a more elaborate sequence (same book: *Space Encounters* Volume I: *Chunking Down the 21ˢᵗ Century*). Setting it up is the text below.

At the outset, I quoted Timothy Ferris's *The Whole Shebang* about an implication of Einstein's general theory of relativity.[10] He explained how in this theory, gravity was a result of warped space. In "curved space, the effects Newton attributes to gravity," he pointed out, "are local, not distant. In general relativity, *the course of any object describes a 'world line,' which is a trajectory through space and time....*" Hmmm. A world line. That got my attention. So, in relativity, gravity is not a "force" but a consequence of—of course, it's the reshaping of space, the bending, warping, curving made by mass/matter.

Next, backstage, the "artist computer" went into overdrive, or perhaps it "went bananas." It was as if lightning struck it and it tore, tossed, poured page after page out of the printer, once I followed up (below) on Ferris's brilliantly simple analysis. If you're already familiar with the story of myself at seven at my first piano recital, sit tight. It's just the means to get the computer going. So here I brought Ferris's comment (on the trajectory in curved space through time) into the picture of the little girl/myself who forgot her recital piece by Johann Sebastian Bach—but continued to attempt to play it by returning to the beginning *and with each attempt remembering more, slowly making her way through note passages, adding new ones with each replay.*

I wrote:

> Returning to the in-depth meaning, the
> gravitational picture, of a young girl sitting at a
> piano, going round and round in an orbit of an unfinished
> memorized note structure. More degrees at each attempt
> at the circumference.

As if orbiting around an unseen pathway or impediment that prevented finishing but signaled the need to continue.

Finally,

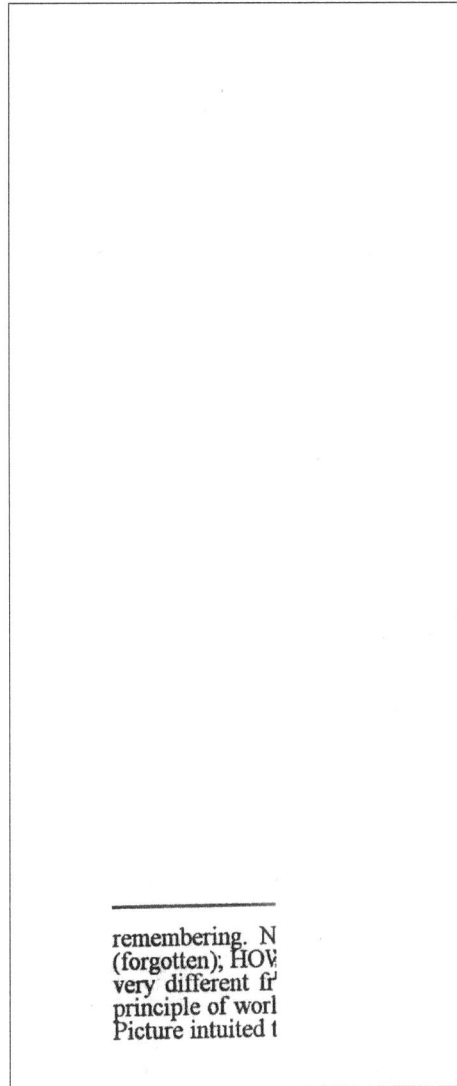

remembering. N
(forgotten); HOV
very different fr
principle of worl
Picture intuited t

remembering. Not

during all the broken-off cycles . . .

14wα‡♥αⓐ♦8wx ~α 8wz ⓢ Ç) Ç@11wx α0ᾁ¬12wy ±Γⓢ◔ (|10wy ⑧0 ⌐

during *all the broken-o*
T ENDED. If you raised i
. a simple Bach barcarol
ines, demonstrating wha
ough the actions of

The baffled computer, unprogrammed, could not do this in the 1990s. Unassisted. Supposedly. Note that the lines go in two directions. So this is fun, isn't it? A mystery right in my own living room. I was swept up in it.

The computer printer reassembled portions of the words on-screen into picture texts. But what was on the screen was quite orderly.

There, I was speculating that what if there were (for the right brain hemisphere, the pictorial mind) symbolic patterns we fell into? That's in addition to physical patterns we all often found ourselves or an event in. And why not? It made sense that they existed.

The on-screen passage that the printouts are re-creating in wild abandon connected the simple act of gradually remembering forgotten piano notes—remembering more and more and more—to the overarching timeline (the "world line"): the "gravitational role" it played, perhaps as a big road sign to a life purpose (or an angle of it). The straight screen text read:

Remembering. Not during all the broken-off cycles—what happened at the end (forgotten). HOW IT ENDED. If you raised it from off the piano into its worldline, very different from a simple Bach barcarolle played literally. From there, to the principle of world lines, demonstrating what would unconsciously carry the Whole Picture intuited through the actions of

NOT STOPPING TILL THE END. That is, the prewritten REAL END. Rather than some arbitrary, local indifferent performance. But a giantly total performance: how could it be connected into

(based on what law???)

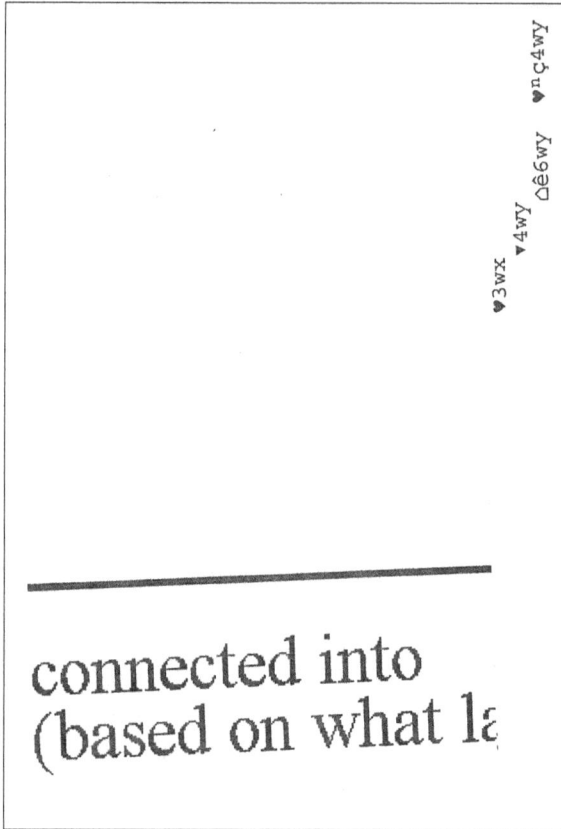

♥3wx ♥4wy △ê6wy ♥nç4wy

connected into
(based on what la

By sitting at the piano, and the unconscious mind going and doing

*b0W

WHAT? WHERE? what carried it into the whole? And monitored (instructed???) the brain to stay in this track? This pattern? AND FROM WHER

⊤◄α◄ü◄01Ç⑨)

E WAS THAT PICKED UP and to .
ıg-range lifetime-shaping significd
/ely but publicly into the whole, of
n, did it have something, by way o

EMONSTRATE. Picking it out slol
erstanding it exemplified, so many¡
ne, saying it all—by NOT STOPPI
   BUT this principle was—by the(
exactly. So we have to see what(
tE reaching the new structure—whe
-ies) will make MUCH MORE S
ıs in going TOWARD the under¡
x. Nearing the other end, howeveı
t expansion and turns back tow.
and—the elementary choice of: TC

E WAS THAT PICKED UP and to what effect? How could a local action have any long-range lifetime-shaping significance, if it did? And how, in going so secretively but publicly into the whole, of time and space, inside not a spaceship but a pattern, did it have something, by way of principle, to

DEMONSTRATE.

The computer responded with a barrage of "signatures," like friends who didn't have names in our sense, but had energy identities they expressed with letters, numbers, symbols. Unfortunately, the *Electricity* book font has changed how the letters fell in the 1990s Times font and early Word Perfect software I used. Just imagine the computer sliced through the original, producing a swath in which the exact original relationships inside the characters were maintained. Further adding complication, these texts were long, running footnotes, thus small to begin with, hard to replicate in a book-width line.

Time out. *How could it happen? Why?* is obvious. *To illustrate the choppy memory, recovering snatches at a time.*

It is perfectly re-creating the broken-offness of the short-circuited memory of The End of my recital piece (standing in for "life story" if you fast-forward the pattern. At least, I am suggesting that. Remember, beneath the subatomic particles, what holds everything together, governing manifestation, might be patterns, according to some physicists.)

The fragmented text captured the memory fragments of starting over and starting over till I remembered The End. AND played it straight through first note to finish. Not bad for seven. A formula, an archetype, I could walk in when needed.

The computer illustration acts out the predicament. Or, as in any good illustration of a story, captures the emotion. More fragments follow. I'll just give an example. A roll of drums:

Hugging the edge of the page, the printout does not make it easy on the scanner. Always two directions, and perching like a bird on a telephone pole right on the top edge here, halfway off.

The point is taken: the Whole broke down. It played out—was lived—in pieces. But there was a Big Picture, behind the fragments.

> Does [the] image of the jigsaw puzzle with a broken symmetry that is momentarily restored by the random configuration of its component parts stand as a metaphor for synchronicity? Clearly not . . . Synchronicity is more than a mere chance arrangement of disconnected parts into a pattern, for it involves a conjunction of the individual and the global, and arises out of some deep principle that binds elements together into a fundamental pattern. . . . Something like symmetry can emerge out of an apparently chaotic ground, in response to some underlying symmetry principle.[11]
>
> —F. David Peat

It was no accident, I am saying, that I got partway down the track or course and started over again. I knew to do that. And got a little further the next time. But turned around and started from the beginning again. No accident because somewhere inside I was "programmed" (my consciousness was messaging me) that giving up was not in the cards for me. But let me illustrate with William Blake. My friend Milton Klonsky was telling me one day how he lived in poverty. I said: "But he never gave up?"

He looked at me in deep communication and replied, heartfelt: *"He gave up over and over again.* But he went on *after* giving up."

In the recital I played a heavenly barcarole by Johan Sebastian Bach. What a marvelous first model to spin one's World Line off of.

The "scraps" of the paragraph I reproduced here do not quite fit together, as there were many many illustrations to go with this passage. Also, not all survived my shipment of boxes from Belgium to the U.S. But this passage—in fact, the several simple paragraphs that told this ostensibly ordinary narrative—produced/inspired a collection of pages to reflect it.

Not enough clues? A barcarolle," a song of Venetian gondoliers—says Merrian Webster—is "usually in $^6/_8$ or $^{12}/_8$ time characterized by the alternation of a strong and weak beat that suggests a rowing rhythm."

at hap
piano,
ally. F
sciousl

45

I detected this as a paradigm: What even a child could understand—the elementary choice of: TO FINISH OR NOT.

Be the predicted final product, visible, walking the Earth, oneself seen in the final moments when the shape of it all—big, tall—through time, is PERMISSIBLE. According to these simple, unwritten laws.

"Be th predicted fnal product,
the final monents when he shape
PERMISSIBLE.According to these simp

You know now. You know now, even as she reached the end, finally—trying over and over. THIS TIME, you know *THE END*.

Q

So now here, in concise sentences, here is the en of the story. Not there, not everywhere, but

he end,
END is.

≡ ▽⊥}WOↃↄ®Ↄ╪╤⌐HW8♠⟩ ⟨⟨⟩⊕πZW6♥◄♦ °∬xↄↄ⟷ƒ

Of course, at that moment I didn't know at all. But someone or something did and the energy flew on and on. It all sounded so real to me, in the 1990s in that spirit-jammed apartment. I might as well have been William Blake holding visitations from 9:00 pm till 5:00 am, though for him it started at age four, when he saw God "put his head to the window." At nine he saw angels in trees. Obviously, it was true. No matter that

I was in the dark.

"Your time is UP. Your time for Recruiting parts of yourself."

How I wrote and counseled my present self those decades ago. Or that self (this me now) made sure I (this me) would get here by outlining how it would happen and what the alternatives were.

When somewhere inside your head comes the message that your time is up, let me tell you you pay attention. Actually, I wrote and wrote it, not knowing when, but since it was "in the present," it felt

✳

At this point in finally writing this book, 2022, I Skyped with my Belgian Tai Chi master/Taoist friend, Jef Crab, who always brings presence into a conversation with me.

"Why do you think the computer PK was possible?" I asked. *(By the way, I only did in those ten years in the 1990s in Belgium. After I returned to the United States, in late 2001, I did not continue it but set a new goal: not to create and pile texts and photography—unseen by others—around me but to bring things out.)*

Over the Skype screen, down in his home in Surinam near the rainforest, on ten acres of land sheltered by the aroma of coffee beans he grows and the thicket of communicating trees, Jef answered, "I have to go back about fifteen billion years."

"In the beginning," he went on, starting with what's familiar, "the Universe was very condensed," referring to the Big Bang. "And it was Light that brought it into being because Light is not only Energy, it's also Information. There are two aspects. Information indicates the direction. The Energy provides the growing force: what transforms the things/objects/organisms. The Big Bang of Light—it created galaxies, stars, the Earth. We know that the Earth was formed out of the Light of the sun, the dust and gas of the Sun Nebula. The Information connected to the Light is what created the first subtle Forms, the only places with a different vibration, in this nebula. Such divergent vibrations become a divergent temperature and attract quantum particles, bringing gasses, etc., . . . into existence.

"All the minerals, plants, animals, humans—all came from it in a similar way." (That's in a nutshell, referring to processes involving accretion, photosynthesis, cooling until the Snowball Earth era, oxygenation, and densification, etc.)

Where does the Information come from?"

"The primordial Light. Information and Energy are Yin and Yang of the Tai Chi." Switching quickly: "Why did the Light create a human being? In my opinion, for us human beings to return to the Light. Similar to what Lao Tzu, the Daoist sage, said: "All must return to its Origin.""

"Then, is the Light consciousness?"

"Consciousness is an attribute of the Soul," Jef answered. Then: "The moment I'm coherent, the Light will connect with me. Meister Eckhart already said that in the thirteenth century: *if I become completely empty of myself, out of his nature God has to fill me (i.e., the Light will fill me).*

"I can only bring myself into that condition from which the Light will connect with me. It's always a grace, a gift from the Light. When I find the correct inner alignment, I reconnect to the primordial Light or Sound. Same thing."

"So what," I asked, "has that to do with my computer PK? For instance, was it Light Beings, spirits playing?"

"You can call it that, as a Light Being is only Information and Energy in a nonmaterial, or subtle, form."

"Synchronicity is bringing us into the Present and offers us a glimpse of Eternity, the very Nature of the Light."

"—into awareness of infinity. The moment I reconnect to the Light, it's like a Big Bang inside myself."

Jef added: "So, just to complete our chat: Every experience of synchronicity is a faint repetition of the Big Bang and of the three moments in life when a human being can connect to the Primordial

Light, i.e., at birth, when dying—both unavoidable—and the third during deep awareness. The latter can be a conscious and even repeated action. For those who do not practice such techniques, synchronicity can be compared to be a fractal of a Mandelbrot symmetry on a psychic/spiritual level. Its real purpose is to wake us up to the existence of the Light and the desire to return to it."

A motto
a principle
for the new era,
of INFORMATION

Not to leave the energy out
Not to shut it out
in bringing in
THE INFORMATION

Information is useless
if bartered for
our freedom
of exploration

o, but very many realized it as such

but information (another voice) isn't to explore
information (original voice) is entirely
to explore
No, IT IS FACTS
NO, it is
SPACE exploration
And so I took an advance step into this new-century issue.

It/I continued: "Now we are threading the archetypal material above the mind of the Earth."

PART THREE

Picking up the (fascinating-to-me) predictions from back then, when the computer PK wafted them in, down to my fingertips, I bask in their relevancy today, now, as I draw closer to wrapping up this existence, this lifetime. I wrote:

at the start here, only at the announcing of the
al of myself, as I try to explain it to myself. No
n in, unless it turns out to be useful by way of
, how such things happen and how they might
structions. Besides, we have not gotten to the
ath: of multiplication, addition, subtraction,
then will we get to CALCULUS???? Everything
jumping to categories of the outer form—the
geocentric; the egocentric. Now, many people
... to explain ...
... this idea already cast out ...
vere thus cast out, of its APPLICATION. Its
c in all the other bodies that interact, the make-
... as ... astronomy ...
... book ... SC ... OF THI
ve isolate the technological from the human, the
astronomical, then we have narrowed down the
... however,
... indeed ...
proved, we would reveal to ourselves all the
... ly; that we say we don't—merely because
... of ...
... out. And we ...

ect. Of the arrival of myself, as I try to e
else has to listen in, unless it turns out t
paring, for them, how such things happe
l upon these instructions. Besides, we h
of human math: of multiplication,
)METRY. And then will we get to CALC
ld be misread if jumping to categories (
forting idea of geocentric; the *ego*centri

I wrote:

I had realized, at last,

that the author of what I had written was not exactly myself, because the author existed inside laws I had not known. By those laws, there were all sorts of ways information could come to reside inside a physical body. . . .

So this I am. I am told this, upon its arrival, I call my birth. That is the only way I can do this, that I have set up a mediumistic self, a writing self, that can communicate in principles what this is that is being described. Else, I do not know how it could be done without confusion as to the integrity of the individual, which this reenforces and takes further, endeavoring to tear down the present barriers and seeming conclusions. No, I never recognize the difficulties that strength could destroy. The strength, passed through, that takes the one who stopped toward the one who did not and cannot relate, except in an anti-self or future self or never-reached self, or extraterrestrial. Or something undefined and nebulous, in the ethers of might-have-been.

I denounce feeble excuses if the wish is real. I denounce the barriers that are pretending, to the one who wished so fervently. Never let the support be doubted if the intent to reach the wish is vigilant and ever-flamed and -torched in the night.

To get myself into myself, these last days, to so shake the molecules that they stood in a new alignment, I had to tear down every structure inside myself. To make every insecurity of the old forms, to break up the sure knowledge of the molecular layers, to tell them all that they had no harmony anymore, to throw out what worked, to step in and hold the magnet of my energy over them, to say this little universe is no more. It is another universal principle, of action inside it. And that principle is myself, the self of yore, of evermore, of the forensic debate over what is and what has value. All this I accumulated to be my signature, my name, though it has no name. I am wordless to say what it is that I am. Only that I express it. And these former alignments sometimes did not feel the power to do so. In entering here, I can come in as no other than myself, that self that is known in other dimensions and that cannot come in in a lesser form. Though albeit I have been said to be in other forms. In truth I can be in no other form at this time. I say all this at this time, to assure that the core has integrity. That it is hard and unyielding. So that the yielding aspects will know how far they can go; that this, which I am, is their boundary, the end of gray area, their eternal no, their recognition and exposing, should it be necessary. But normally, it is enough to say this. And let the courage that then builds do all the rest,

Thus, I could not come until it was certain that I was wanted and asked for and that a place would be held. Because I could do nothing than destroy the place I inhabited if it did not accommodate myself. Rebel against the very walls that were called me. Or that I found myself in. That was hypothetical. It was an abstraction. Naturally, it was imaginary if these rules that govern these energies were unknown. Thus, I come in in an explanation of these rules and these energies—known, of course, spoken of and written of. Yet they did not apply themselves in ways left for me to do, a small space. Quite enough. I do not ask more. I only ask to be me where I am.

For my eyes alone, this writing all made sense then. And more now. Jef just told me (2022) that I will go through a medical issue I am facing. "Will I still be me?" "Yes," he said, "you'll still be you. Only closer to the Light."

Screeching to a halt on racing heels, a new predicament appeared in my life, or tumbled in, and it had the effect—say, purpose—of making me bring out the three short books I was working on, holding back on, loving the spirit energy that was bombarding me with them in 2021–2022. I am bringing them out now in a span of a couple of months, forced out of me under the pressure of knowing I have a medical issue. Supposedly one that will turn out fine. Yea. Fine because I got the message.

However, it's a warning, not to hold within what is a Gift, trying to come out. And so it is.

In this book are a miniscule assortment of the variety of creations of the computer PK and the messages embedded in them I received and piled in a plethora into my apartment in Belgium in the '90s. The playground of a spirit dance, the light-hearted style of particles and fields whirling like dervishes, encountering, holding on, letting go. I would like to dig into my files and pull out some more. It is overwhelming, the voice, the complex messages, the computer PK. Maybe, though, a taste first. A pointer to my Space Encounters *books, which are packed with examples. I have used some samples that are not in those books, some that are, some from three unpublished Space Encounters manuscripts I drafted like running from wildfire just before departing Belgium. A manic computer loading me up. But in those books, carefully published in Romania, it's always original pages that were scanned. Here, it's sometimes scans of photocopies. Stirring the pot to point back to the Light hovering like a spaceship over my computer.*

Passing through New York City, I was talking with my good friend and onetime teacher George Stade, professor in the Department of English and Comparative Literature at Columbia University for thirty-six years.

"What should I do about all this crazy material?"

I was wondering how to be believable, which I no longer find an issue. But it concerned me then. Truth has its own defenses if left to itself.

"Nabokov," he told me whimsically, "would have written it.

"And said he made the whole thing up."

NOTES

1 Omeow, "ELI5: How Does Light or Electricity Carry Information?" https://www.reddit.com/r/explainlikeimfive/comments/42br3q/eli5_how_does_light_or_electricity_carry/

2 "Light Energy," Solar Schools, https://www.solarschools.net/knowledge-bank/energy/types/light.

3 Deepak Chopra, "A Conversation: Consciousness and the Connection to the Universe," April 7, 2012, https://www.sfgate.com/opinion/chopra/article/A-conversation-consciousness-and-the-connection-2464153.php.

4 Tibi Puiu, "Is Information the Fifth State of Matter? Physicist Says There's One Way to Find Out, https://www.zmescience.com/science/news-science/information-energy-mass-eq uivalence/#:-:text= In%2020 1 9%2C%20physicist%20Melvin%20 Vopson,a%20finite%20and%20quantifiable%20mass.

5 The Physics Classroom, https://physicsclassroom.com.

6 "Information Theory: The Information Universe," http://www.thenegativepsychologist.com/information-universe/

7 Y. Elskens and I. Prigogine, "From Instability to Irreversibility," *Proceedings of the National. Academy of Sciences* USA, vol. 83, Aug. 1986, Physics: 5756–5760, contributed by I. Prigogine March 11, 1986, https://www.pnas.org/doi/10.1073/pnas.83.16.5756.

8 "Information Theory: The Information Universe

9 Sarah Charley, "What's Really Happening during HLC Collision?" June 30, 2017, https://www.symmetrymagazine.org/article/whats-really-happening-during-an-lhc-collision.

10 Timothy Ferris, *The Whole Shebang,* New York: Simon & Schuster (1997), 74-75.

11 F. David Peat, *Synchronicity: The Bridge between Mind and Matter*, New York: Bantam Books, 91–92.

Acknowledgments

"And said he made the whole thing up."

I am thankful for too much—practically everything—which all in overt and quiet support both got me through the recent difficult time as I raced in spurts to get this book completed. Having never before formally thanked my North Carolina Dance Institute family for going out of the way to keep me in the best spirits possible, thinking with a like mind, and also uplifting me in dance, let me start here. As always, thankful for meeting Virginia Parrott Williams at Duke, whose insightful eye guided me through many of my earlier books. For Didi-Ionel Cenuşer, who with invincible fortitude and humor formatted and published the *Love in Transition* and *Space Encounters* books in Romania, showing me how to Scotch tape the computer PK creations (not laughing at them) onto film paper for offset printing. For lifelong friends, champions of the Earth and its indigenous teachings, Jyoti and Russell Park, as well as Pui Harvey (all with PhD beside their names and warmth in their hearts); thankful for my friends in Belgium and in New York City and those at Kayumari. For the friends I met after moving back to Raleigh, North Carolina. The marvelous new openings they showed me, including that Alice Osborn laboriously and lovingly curated *Particle Piñata Poetry*. For Jef Crab, who counseled me and raised my spirits. For friends in the Gonzo world, who unexpectedly opened wide their hearts, minds, art, and friendship to me. I particularly thank Ron Whitehead for barreling in, in his total huge energy, to support me in these recent three book projects, an indispensable advisor, offering valuable me, including that Alice Osborn laboriously and lovingly curated *Particle Piñata Poetry*. For Jef Crab, who counseled me and raised my spirits. For friends in the Gonzo world, who unexpectedly opened wide their hearts, minds, art, and friendship to me. I particularly thank Ron Whitehead for barreling in, in his total huge energy, to support me in these recent three book projects, an indispensable advisor, offering valuable suggestions. And family, most notably my sisters, nephew, niece and nephew-in law, and cousin Noel Baucom.

And of course I give grateful acknowledgment for the invaluable, spectacular, contributions of interior designer Deborah Perdue and artist Grant Goodwine, the cover designer.

Especially in this book, I need to thank the spirit world energy that produced some of the content. And tons of energy. It overturned some of my preconceptions and blasted me with the most welcome, fascinating demonstrations of "the light that outshines a thousand suns." And that's just the start. Thanks for the privilege of this lifetime.

Praise for Margaret Harrell's Books

The *Keep This Quiet!* Series

Keep This Quiet! I

"Addictive" and "a delight."
—Mark Strand, former U.S. Poet Laureate

"Margaret Harrell's *Keep This Quiet!* offers an illuminating look at Hunter S. Thompson in full throttle trying to make it as a Top Notch prose-stylist. Harrell fills in many important biographical gaps. A welcome addition to what is becoming the HST cottage industry. Read it."
—Douglas Brinkley, editor of *The Proud Highway* and *Fear and Loathing in America*

"Memoir will likely please Hunter S. Thompson fans and appeal to readers with an interest in the beginnings of the post-modern era or the personal sacrifices involved in bringing serious written work to fruition."
—*Kirkus Indie Reviews*

"With a solid dose of humor and another perspective on these writers from a personal friend, *Keep This Quiet!* is a moving read and much recommended to any literary studies or memoir collection."
—*Midwest Book Review*

"KEEP THIS QUIET! a memoir: *My Relationship with Hunter S. Thompson, Milton Klonsky, and Jan Mensaert* by Margaret A. Harrell is a masterpiece! I never expected to say that about a memoir."
—Ron Whitehead, outlaw poet

"In the ever-expanding list of biographies and memoirs about Hunter S. Thompson, this latest offering, *Keep This Quiet!* by Margaret A. Harrell, is quite simply a breath of fresh air. . . . What sets *Keep This Quiet!* apart is the extent to which Harrell explores the question of identity and myth, in her quest to simultaneously answer questions concerning her own character and that of one Hunter S. Thompson. As Harrell writes early on—"Who was he? There was no indication how complicated that answer was."

—Rory Feehan, PhD, owner of https://totallygonzo.org

"Three men, embodiments of three different dimensions of the late 1960's Zeitgeist—wispy dissolution, language-charged intellect, and Gonzo persona-building—are brought together by Harrell to invoke a world of passion and commitment . . . *Keep This Quiet!* is at once noisy, sensual, and word-drunk, as well as quietly intimate and full of Harrell's wonder at her luck. While most readers will come to this book for the Thompson content, in truth all the portraits here—all four of them—are compelling and often touching."

— W. C. Bamberger, *Rain Taxi Review*

"This is no ordinary book about or including Thompson. It's a memoir detailing personal relationships with three authors, the main focus being on Hunter. . . . [I] must stress that this book, as a memoir is quite deep and holds the door open for the reader. While Hunter is a huge selling point, the book has the legs to stand alone."

—Martin Flynn, owner of https://hstbooks.org

Keep THIS Quiet Too!

"A passionately written memoir that doesn't sit around being fit and proper and straight-laced. If I can use a well-worn phrase here, 'it lifts the lid on so many things.' . . . As a key to the lives of these three writers it is idiosyncratic and in age where blandness is the norm it is a pleasure to go on her journey and find out a little about what made these men tick and what drove her to them."

—*Beat Scene* (UK print magazine)

Keep This Quiet! III

"This is the third and highly recommended title in Margaret Harrell's outstanding *Keep This Quiet!* autobiographical series. A fascinating and very well written personal story, *Keep This Quiet!* III: *Initiations* is very highly recommended for both community and academic library collections. Also exceptionally commended are the first two volumes in this outstanding series, *Keep This Quiet! My Relationship with Hunter S. Thompson, Milton Klonsky, and Jan Mensaert*, and *Keep THIS Quiet Too!*"

—*Midwest Book Review*

Keep This Quiet! IV

"As though it arrived with a full legion of angelic messengers and masters of light, from the moment I touched this book, its energy began to flow through me. If you are ready to welcome energetic shifts toward enlightenment, this book is for you. This beautifully written volume of wisdom provides attunements as you meander through its pages joining Margaret on her journey."

—Diana Henderson, author of *Grandfather Poplar*

"Margaret Harrell's blending and merging the whole of a human being and beyond into the cosmos is astounding writing and what a lifetime Journey she has taken to arrive to this book. I feel Margaret is zipping around and catching the flavors of the world, the universe and Beyond. She is working with a whole new and different combined East-West and Middle Paradigm."

—Suzanne V. Brown, PhD, psychologist, former VP, Exceptional Human Experience

"Margaret Harrell is a skilled professional writer with excellent ability to communicate and weave esoteric ideas about science, psychology, philosophy, and spirituality. Richard Unger's channeled hand analysis description of her as a 'grand synthesizer' was apt and accurate."

—Ron Rattner, author of the forthcoming *From Litigation to Meditation: An ex-lawyer's spiritual metamorphosis from secular Hebrew to born again Hindu to uncertain Undo*

The Hell's Angels *Letters: Hunter S. Thompson, Margaret Harrell and the* Making of an American Classic
(available only at Norfolk Press): https://norfolkpress.com/

"Thompson's motto might well have been 'Nothing in moderation.' For *The Hell's Angels Letters*, Margaret Ann Harrell—in collaboration with Ron Whitehead—has assembled a dossier of all her correspondence with Thompson during the time she worked as the editor of the gonzo writer's 'strange and terrible saga of the outlaw motorcycle gangs.' Typed manuscript pages, scribbled notes, photographs, interviews and all sorts of period ephemera relating to *Hell's Angels* allow the reader a valuable, behind-the-scenes glimpse into the making of this classic of New Journalism."

—Michael Dirda, the *Washington Post*

"As the title implies, this book is mainly comprised of letters between Harrell and Thompson, some typed and some handwritten, and all printed here in colour. Of course, there are already two collections of Hunter Thompson's letters available, but somehow they are even more enjoyable when read in the original form. Whether typed or scrawled in giant letters with a red pen, Thompson's correspondence is invariably annotated and corrected in his unique way, adding a layer of personality that was missing from the collections, as well— of course—as Harrell's explanations that provide further insight."

—David Wills, *Beatdom*

"This is a big book, literally and figuratively." He went on:

> *The Hell's Angels Letters* is a must-have text for any Hunter S. Thompson fan. Lavishly documented and illustrated with the actual correspondence that led to the publication of his breakthrough literary effort, *Hell's Angels*, this coffee-table book literally shows how HST boot-strapped his way from a impoverished nobody journalist to growing legend. The author, Margaret Harrell, who was Thompson's editor on his inaugural book, and her collaborator, Thompson's friend and associate poet Ron Whitehead, have succeeded brilliantly to create a fabulous present for you, or anyone in your life who admires Thompson's numerous achievements. It is not inexpensive, but

no matter, it's worth every penny. *The* Hell's Angels *Letters: Hunter S Thompson, Margaret Harrell and the Making of an American Classic* gets five stars out of five! Bravo!

—Kyle K. Mann, Gonzo Today

Particle Piñata Poems

"The time of the grandmothers, of the nurturing healing feminine energy has arrived. Patriarchy has sewn destruction long enough. We must all, female and male, become healers, seers. In her epic PARTICLE PIÑATA, author Margaret Ann Harrell stands in direct lineage with the desert mystics, the poet prophets of old and, simultaneously, with the contemporary cutting edge avant-garde. In a whirling dance with the creative forces of the universe Harrell draws explicit and implicit lines to Rumi, Blake, Yeats, Joyce, Jung, and others while forging mystical connections with clouds and coastlines, dancing in the borderlands of space and time, of being and not being, of embracing and letting go. And she accomplishes it all in her own distinctly original poetic voice. Through decades of carrying these poems from continent to continent, Margaret Ann Harrell has continued to add new poems and photos, to edit and revise, to transform her self into an ever evolving being, into this masterpiece book. I can't recommend it highly enough. Go ahead, open the front cover and enter. You'll never be the same."

—Ron Whitehead, U.S. National Beat Poet Laureate

"The poetry of Margaret Ann Harrell reads like a Zhuangzi of the 21st century, taking its reader through a spiritual Odyssey, where one can hear the cosmic beat in the rhythm of the word play, the pulse of heartfelt mind blowing experiences revealing a vast span of messages from beyond. It shows the craftmanship of a female shaman who has the power to catch such a dazzling wild and free roaming content into the nets of poems. Here is a biopic in words, a biographical epic, a story of a lifetime full of surprising leaps into the story of Earth and the Cosmic Drama, a rite de passage (read the passage) initiating its reader into multiversal dimensions, bringing meaning to life where few have been looking to find it. This great bold poetry full of wit and spirit reads as a unique treat, a gift from those who know how to sow the seed for what really matters on earth: a choice to live a life guided by love and light. For those who are in love with poetry, share this genuine gift and the sheer joy of it! If you want to, go ahead!"

—Chris Van de Velde (MA Philosophy, lover of wisdom), Belgium.

Cloud Conversations & Image Stories—Leonardo's Theory

"This is Margaret Harrell's gift, . . . the images and the writing that goes with them. . . . She is an energy manifester and she's bringing it through these energies. . . . This is not only an artbook, it's not only an intellectual book, it's about raising consciousness. . . . [The images are] something uniquely different . . . aren't in the Earth archetypes."

—Mariah Martin, Founder of Light Path Enterprises, reviewing similar images in *Toward a Philosophy of Perception*

Also by Margaret A. Harrell

Cloud Conversations & Image Stories—Leonardo's Theory

Particle Piñata Poems

The Hell's Angels *Letters: Hunter S. Thompson, Margaret Harrell and the Making of an American Classic*—in collaboration with Ron Whitehead

Keep This Quiet!

Keep THIS Quiet Too!

Keep This Quiet! III

Keep This Quiet! IV, rev. ed.

Toward a Philosophy of Perception: The Magnitude of Human Potential—Cloud Optics

Marking Time with Faulkner—Literary Criticism

Space Encounters volumes I–III

Love in Transition volumes I–IV

About the Author

Margaret Ann Harrell was born in North Carolina and educated academically at Duke University (BA) and Columbia University (MA). She did postgraduate work at the C. G. Jung Institute in Zurich (1984–'87), followed by energy studies and investigations that continue to this day. After thirty adventurous years abroad in Morocco and Europe, in late 2001 she moved back to the United States. Since that time, she has been an advanced-meditation lightbody teacher—most recently a luminous-body teacher—in the Orin & DaBen LuminEssence work.

Margaret was a copyeditor/assistant editor at Random House, New York City, often to first-book writers who later became prominent, such as Hunter S. Thompson. Introduced to parapsychology by J. B. Rhine at Duke University, she eventually found a part of her calling in exploring the meaning and boundaries of consciousness/unconsciousness. She is a three-time fellow at MacDowell Colony.

Margaret is in demand as a speaker. Most recently, at the Canessa Gallery in San Francisco in July 2021 for the launch of *The* Hell's Angels *Letters: Hunter S. Thompson, Margaret Harrell and the Making of an American Classic*, in collaboration with Ron Whitehead, US National Beat Poet Laureate. With noted contributors and reviewers, including the *Washington Post*, this high-end coffee table paperback is available only at the website of the publisher, Norfolk Press of San Francisco. Earlier, she authored the four-volume memoir series *Keep This Quiet!* (Saeculum University Press 2011–'18). And before that, published in Sibiu, Romania, in English, the seven-volume nonfiction *Love in Transition* and *Space Encounters* series.

In cloud photography, exhibited in Romania, Italy, Belgium, and New York City, she is fascinated with the sun. Her biography and photographs were also many times in Marquis *Who's Who in Modern American Art*. For several years she has given VIP presentations at the Gonzofest (Louisville) and presented at the Carolina Book and Writers Conference. Margaret, a longtime freelance book editor, now edits additionally but not exclusively for authors in the Self-Publishing School. For a fuller picture, see https://margaretharrell.com.

Thank You for Reading My Book

Authors live by readers and their reviews. If you enjoyed *Electricity*
"Transport Trains"— slipping information under our noses into our lives,
I would deeply appreciate an honest positive review on Amazon
and/or other platform. I will read every
word you write and benefit from the comments.

Thank you again and God bless.

www.ingramcontent.com/pod-product-compliance
Lightning Source LLC
Chambersburg PA
CBHW060255030426
42335CB00014B/1715